# Saints of the California Missions

## Norman Neuerburg

On the front cover is Saint Anthony of Padua by José de Páez, now at Mission San Miguel. Left: Our Lady of Guadalupe, the patroness of the Americas. In the 1830s, Franciscan friars from the College of Guadalupe in Zacatecas, Mexico, came to northern California to relieve the aging friars from the College of San Fernando. Diego Garcia, the first Bishop of Both Californias, was from the College of Guadalupe and he founded the first college in California in 1845 at Santa Inés. His college was also dedicated to Our Lady of Guadalupe. Above: the statue of the Archangel Gabriel from the main altar of his mission; Mexico, 1791.

# The Saints of the California Missions

Visitors to California are often struck by the abundance of saints among the placenames throughout the state. This, of course, dates back to the time of Spanish and Mexican rule when the names of the saints of the day were often applied to newly discovered localities, whether rivers, bays, mountains, or valleys. Saints' names were also usually chosen for most permanent establishments such as presidios or forts, pueblos or towns, and, of course, the Franciscan missions. Here, however, greater care was taken beyond the simple happenstance of the day when the establishment was founded. The choice of the patron theoretically was the privilege of the Viceroy, though it was certainly in concert with the ecclesiastical authorities in the case of the missions. In fact, one might question how much choice the Viceroy really had here; he certainly would not impose a saint contrary to the wishes of the Fathers.

The patrons are all typically Spanish ones; some are Franciscan favorites and even specifically Majorcan Franciscan ones. Of the twenty-one dedications one third, seven, are Franciscan friars, one a Franciscan nun; three are members of the Third Order of Saint Francis; two are early Christian virgin martyrs, and the rest are scriptural. All of the missions with Franciscan patrons, except San Francisco Solano, were founded during Serra's time, and he had hoped for a mission for that saint from the beginning. All but three of the patrons could be found among the paintings in the choir or on the altars of the church of the Monastery of San Francisco in Palma de Mallorca where Fray Junípero Serra resided for many years. Most of them also appear on the altars of the Franciscan church of San Bernardino in Petra, Serra's birthplace. The Spaniards had a special devotion to the Immaculate Conception but the Majorcans even more so. Saint Bonaventure was a great proponent of the belief in the Immaculate Conception, and that explains the surprising number of his images in the California missions. In Majorca, however, when he is shown with the Immaculate Conception he is most frequently paired with the Blessed Ramon Llull, though that learned worthy never made it to the altars of California.

The choice of Saint Charles Borromeo as patron of the second mission and presidio certainly was in homage to the Spanish King Carlos III, just as San Fernando not only referred to the Spanish royal line, but was also patron of the College in Mexico City that supplied missionaries to California.

The images of the saints of the Roman Catholic church, whether two-dimensional or three, served a double function in the California missions as visual aids and as objects of devotion. They served as examples to teach the new converts about the heroes of Christian belief and to inspire prayer to the Supreme Being through the intercession of his special workers.

In the following pages we shall endeavor to recount something about these saints, their lives, and why they were popular. After discussing the development of their iconography in the history of art we shall indicate what images of them once were found in the California missions and what now survives. Our illustrations will be taken from paintings and sculptures now in the missions which are known to have been there in the early days.

Paradise, 18th century Mexican painting sent to Mission San Antonio in 1786, now at Mission San Miguel

# San Diego de Alcalá

San Diego de Alcalá, Saint Didacus of Alcalá, became patron of the bay which now bears his name in 1602 when Captain Sebastián Vizcaíno arrived on November 12th, the eve of the saint's feast day. The flagship was also named in his honor. The name was subsequently applied to Alta California's first mission by Fray Junípero Serra on July 16th, 1769, and to the presidio.

Diego was born of humble parents in the Andalusian village of San Nicolás del Puerto near Seville around 1400. Early on he was attracted to the spiritual life and lived with a hermit before entering the Franciscan order as a brother at Arrizafa near Córdova. He was sent to the Canary Islands as a missionary and was so successful that he was chosen as guardian of the Franciscan community on the Island of Fuerteventura from 1445 to 1449. In 1450 he accompanied Fr. Alonzo de Castro to Rome to attend the canonization of Saint Bernardine of Siena. While in Rome he resided at the monastery of Santa Maria in Aracoeli on the Capitoline Hill where he took care of the sick and was credited with miraculous cures. In time he returned to Spain and worked in the infirmary of the great University of Alcalá in Castille. He died there in 1463 and is buried under the high altar of the cathedral. He was canonized by the Franciscan Pope Sixtus V in 1588. Diego had a special devotion to the Cross. He was especially concerned with feeding the poor, even giving away food of the monastery. Once he was reprimanded by his superiors for this and was asked to open his habit to reveal the bread he had taken only to have it transformed into roses. Traditionally the Cross and roses and bread are his attributes, and one or more of these symbols appear in most representations of him.

He was a popular subject in Spanish art of the seventeenth century, and there are works of him by such distinguished painters as Murillo, Ribera, and Zubarán, and the sculptors Alonso Cano and Pedro de Mena. A chapel dedicated to him in the church of San Giacomo degli Spagnuoli (Saint James of the Spaniards) in Rome was adorned with frescoes by Annibale Carracci and Francesco Albani; a chapel also was dedicated to him in the church of Santa Maria in Aracoeli, commemorating his stay there.

In California paintings and sculptures of him seem to have been limited to the mission and presidio of San Diego. Both had statues of him. A painting had been destined for the mission as early as 1769, though it did not arrive until 1772; it was damaged in the revolt of 1775. A large painting which had arrived by 1777 was used temporarily in the chapel of the presidio, while a third, smaller painting was sent in 1782. All three show the saint with both the Cross and the roses. The first painting was recently restored after being returned to Mission San Diego; a second is now at Mission San Luis Rey, while the third is on loan to the Serra Museum in San Diego.

SAINT DIDACUS OF ALCALÁ by José de Páez, sent to Mission San Diego in 1772 and recently returned to Mission San Diego.

# San Luis Rey de Francia

San Luis Rey de Francia, Saint Louis King of France, was chosen by the Vicerory, the Marquis de Branciforte, as the patron of the eighteenth California mission, partially to recognize the relationship of France and Spain through the House of Bourbon. It was founded on June 13, 1798, by the Father Presidente, Fray Fermín Francisco de Lasuén.

Louis IX, King of France, was the son of Louis VIII and Blanche of Castille, sister of Saint Ferdinand, King of Spain; he was born in 1215 at Poissy. His father died when he was eleven, and his mother ruled as regent until he came of age. He was an active and just ruler. Preferring peace to war he chose to negotiate when possible but undertook battle when necessary. He led two crusades; one to Egypt in 1248-1249 ended with his imprisonment. A second one, to Tunis in 1270, resulted in his death from pestilence. He led a righteous and holy life, giving to the poor and spending much time in prayer. He was a member of the Third Order of Saint Francis and eventually came to be considered their patron. He caused the Sainte-Chapelle in Paris to be built to house the relic of the Crown of Thorns given to him by Baldwin, Emperor of Constantinople, in 1239. He was canonized in 1297.

Saint Louis is usually represented in royal garb, often over armor, wearing a crown and with a sceptre sometimes topped with a fleur-de-lis in his right hand. His left hand may hold a sword, an orb, or the Crown of Thorns. In the earlier centuries he is usually smooth-shaven, but in the seventeenth and eighteenth centuries, especially in Spanish countries, he is bearded. Until the nineteenth century, narrative scenes tended to be limited to those showing him giving alms to the poor. He has a place on the Altars of the Kings in New World cathedrals. His popularity, not surprisingly, was great in France; he is the patron of the French national church in Rome, San Luigi dei Francesi, and of the cathedrals of New Orleans and Saint Louis in those areas of French colonization now in the United States. As his mother was Spanish he had some following in Spain, particularly in royal foundations, but devotion to him is most closely connected with the Third Order of Saint Francis.

Representations of him in California were rare. A painting of him was billed to the Monterey presidio in 1791. A painting apparently arrived for the founding of his mission, but the statue for the main altar came only in 1808. A statue, now lost, once occupied the niche in the upper part of the facade of the mission church at least until 1850 but had disappeared by 1856.

SAINT LOUIS KING OF FRANCE, sent to Mission San Luis Rey in 1808 and recently returned there.

# San Juan Capistrano

San Juan de Capistrano (the original form), Saint John of Capestrano, was chosen as patron of the seventh mission by the Viceroy Bucareli. A first foundation on October 30, 1775, was abandoned because of the Indian revolt in San Diego. The mission was again founded on November 1, 1776, by Fray Junípero Serra. The saint's name had, however, first been applied to the valley where Mission San Luis Rey was eventually founded.

John was born in the village of Capestrano in the mountains of the Abruzzi in central Italy in 1385. His father was said to have been a German baron, and his mother belonged to the local nobility. As a youth he studied law in the University of Perugia, and in 1412 he married a local lady and was named governor of the city by King Ladislaus of Naples. He was sent as an emissary to mediate peace in a war with the Malatesta family but ended up in prison. His experiences led him to take holy orders as a Franciscan in 1416, his wife having died or consented to his ordination. He studied under Bernardine of Siena and became a close follower of his. When he became a priest he was a powerful preacher and was sent by the pope all over Europe. In 1455 he organized a crusade against the newly victorious Turks and led a Christian army and turned them back at Belgrade in 1456. He died of a fever not long after the victory. He had founded a monastery in his native city but left before construction was far along. He was beatified in 1690 and canonized in 1724.

His devotion was especially popular in the Austro-Hungarian empire. He is usually shown in a Franciscan habit and may wear a breastplate. He usually carries a banner with a cross and either a crucifix or a sword. He may also carry a plaque with the monogram of Jesus which was popularized by his mentor Saint Bernardine of Siena. His representations in both painting and sculpture are generally limited to Franciscan churches, and there are a few works by major artists which represent him.

In California his mission had a number of representations. At the founding a print had to serve, but a painting which had been ordered by Fr. Serra in 1775 arrived in 1776 and now hangs in the new church of the mission. It is a work by José de Páez, as was requested, and he wears a breastplate and carries both flag and sword. Statues were sent in 1790, 1794, and 1803. The last, like the painting, has the breastplate and carried both sword and flag. It is probably the statue which early in this century was transformed into Saint Anthony of Padua. The only other image in a California mission is a statue on one of the side altars in the church of Mission Dolores which came in 1810. He wears a breastplate and carries a sword and a crucifix.

SAN JUAN CAPISTRANO.

SAINT JOHN OF CAPESTRANO by José de Páez, ordered in 1775 for Mission San Juan Capistrano by Fr. Serra, now in new parish church.

# San Gabriel Arcángel

San Gabriel Arcángel, Saint Gabriel the Archangel, was the patron of the fourth mission which was founded September 4th, 1771. The choice of the dedication had been made by the Viceroy Carlos Francisco de Croix the previous summer.

The Archangel Gabriel - his name means Strength of God - is one of the three angels mentioned by name in the Bible. In the Old Testament he appears twice in the Book of Daniel and in the New Testament he announces the birth of John the Baptist to Zacharias and the birth of Jesus to Mary.

He is most frequently represented in art from early Christian times as a winged figure, often holding a lily representing purity, bringing the message of the Incarnation to the Virgin Mary who is often kneeling and shown with a prayer book. In the art of the Eastern Church he is often shown as a separate figure, perhaps paired with Michael. Throughout the history of Christian art few artists failed to represent the Annunciation at one time or another. The subject appears in both two-and three-dimensional form.

In California the Archangel Gabriel appears both in sculpture and painting. There were canvases of the Annunciation at San Gabriel, San Juan Capistrano, and San Fernando missions, but none of those original ones appears to have survived. Paintings of just the archangel can be seen at San Gabriel and San Miguel (originally from San Antonio) while he is included with two other archangels in a fine painting in the church of Mission Santa Bárbara. Statues from Mexico can now be seen at San Gabriel and San Luis Rey on the reredos and in the museum at Santa Bárbara mission.

He is principally a messenger from God bringing enlightenment, an announcer of our good works to God, and of our arrival in heaven, and is a protector of small children. Devotion to him was not particularly strong in California however, in comparison to the other two archangels.

THE ARCHANGEL GABRIEL, 18th century Mexican painting formerly at Mission San Antonio, now at Mission San Miguel.

# San Fernando Rey de España

San Fernando Rey de España, Saint Ferdinand King of Spain, was chosen as the patron of the seventeenth California mission by the Viceroy, the Marquis de Branciforte. It was founded on September 8, 1797, the fourth that year, by the Father Presidente, Fray Fermín Francisco de Lasuén. San Fernando was also the patron of the Franciscan college in Mexico City which sent the missionaries to California.

Ferdinand, the third Spanish king of that name, was born at Salamanca in 1198. His father was Alfonso IX, King of León, and his mother was Berengaria, daughter of Alfonso III, King of Castille. Through his mother he inherited that title while his father still reigned over León. Eventually Ferdinand became king of the united kingdoms of Castille and León, the symbols of which are on the Spanish royal arms. His sister was Blanche of Castille, mother of Saint Louis King of France. He proved to be a very good ruler, showing great compassion for his subjects and avoiding overburdening them with taxation. He successfully carried out campaigns against the Mohammedans, eventually expelling them from all of Spain except Granada and Alicante. He conquered Córdova and Seville and transformed their great mosques into cathedrals of the Blessed Virgin. He lived an exemplary life, stressing humility and prayer. He was a member of the Third Order of Saint Francis. He founded the University of Salamanca. After his death in 1252 he was buried in the simple habit of the Third Order in the Cathedral of Seville. Many miracles were said to have been performed at his tomb. He was canonized in 1671 by Clement X. In 1717 his remains were placed in a magnificent reliquary of gold-plated silver and crystal above the altar of the Royal Chapel.

Saint Ferdinand is usually shown as a king with a crown and wearing a breastplate beneath robes of ermine; he may hold a sceptre and orb. Representations of him are rare before the seventeenth century, though some by Zurbarán and Murillo antedate his canonization. The eighteenth century Spanish kings made much of him even putting the Academy of Fine Arts under his patronage. In Mexico and South America he joins other kingly saints on Altars of the Kings usually placed behind the main altar in cathedrals as in Mexico City, Puebla, and Cuzco.

His representations in California were rare. A rollable canvas of him was billed to the Monterey Presidio in 1791, the year after a church in Madrid was dedicated to the saint by King Carlos IV. According to an inventory of 1808 the church at San Fernando mission had both a painting and a life-size statue of the patron. The statue is still there, but the painting appears to have been gone by 1849, the date of the last inventory of the mission.

SAINT FERDINAND KING OF SPAIN, statue on the high altar of Mission San Fernando, sent from Mexico in 1808.

# San Buenaventura

San Buenaventura, Saint Bonaventure, had been intended by the Inspector General Don José de Gálvez to be the third of the missions, but its founding was repeatedly delayed until March 31st, 1782, making it the ninth of the missions.

Bonaventure was born Giovanni di Fidanza in the village of Bagnorea near Viterbo in the hills north of Rome, in 1221. The name Bonaventure was given to him, according to a pious legend, after Saint Francis healed the four-year-old boy and exclaimed "O! Buona ventura!" (Good fortune). As a youth he demonstrated a particular zeal for learning and eventually took his degree at the Sorbonne in Paris at the same time as the Dominican Saint Thomas Aquinas. Bonaventure had entered the Franciscan order in 1238 or 1243. He was elected minister general of the order and did much to reform and clear up internal problems among feuding groups. In 1265 he refused the archbishopric of York but became cardinal bishop of Albano in 1273 in order to aid Pope Gregory X in organizing the council to discuss the reunion of the Eastern and Western churches. He was very effective in reconciling differences but died in 1274 before the council was concluded. He was noted as a superb philosopher and theologian, one of the finest minds of the century, and was a prolific writer. He was buried in Lyons where the council was held, though his remains were later desecrated by the Huguenots. He was canonized in 1482 and was declared a Doctor of the Church by Sixtus V in 1588.

He is usually shown wearing the Franciscan habit, sometimes with a surplice and a cardinal's cloak. He may be bareheaded or wear a bishop's mitre, a cardinal's hat, or the biretta of a Doctor of Philosophy. He is most frequently shown with a book and a pen and occasionally carries a model of a church. Representations of him are not rare but usually are found in Franciscan churches where he was venerated for his learning.

His mission had two statues of him of which one is still on the main altar; a painting signed by José de Páez, perhaps the gift of the King, is also owned by the mission. A half-length representation of him once belonged to a family in the town and may also have been at the mission. Other statues of him can still be seen at Carmel, San Antonio, San Gabriel, and San José. Ones, now lost, were at La Purísima and San Luis Rey. Those at San Gabriel and San Luis Rey were paired with his friend Saint Thomas Aquinas. Among paintings the one now at San Miguel appears to have come from San Antonio and one at Santa Bárbara is not identified before the 1858 inventory, though it could well have come at an earlier date. A painting now at Carmel does not appear to be the one mentioned in an invoice of 1774.

SAINT BONAVENTURE, 18th century Mexican painting, formerly at Mission San Antonio and now at Mission San Miguel.

# Santa Bárbara Virgen y Mártir

Santa Bárbara Virgen y Mártir, Saint Barbara Virgin and Martyr, was chosen as the patron of the tenth of the California missions. It was founded on the saint's day, December 4th, 1786, one of only three missions where the date of founding coincided with the saint's day. The name had been given to the channel by Vizcaíno in 1602 and subsequently to the presidio in 1782.

Barbara, according to tradition, was the daughter of a certain pagan Dioscorus in Nicomedia during the time of the emperor Maximian. He kept her shut up in a tower until she should marry. She secretly was converted to Christianity and refused her father's candidate for a spouse. While he was away on a voyage he left orders for a bath structure to be built for her which was to be attached to the tower; she caused three windows symbolizing the Trinity to be included. Upon her father's return he discovered her conversion and resolved to execute her himself. After he carried his deed out he was struck by lightning and died. The oldest known version of the legend dates from the tenth century, though her popularity dates from the seventh. She was especially popular in the Middle Ages and became the patron saint of fireworks makers, artillerymen, architects, founders, stonemasons, gravediggers, fortifications, and magazines and was the protectress against lightning, fire, sudden death, and impenitence. She was eliminated from the Calendar of Saints after the Second Vatican Council because her existence was considered highly dubious. Nonetheless her devotion continues on a popular level.

In art she is usually shown holding the palm of martyrdom and is accompanied by a tower, usually with three windows, which she may carry as a model; she may also carry a chalice or even a monstrance. She often wears the crown of a princess. Images of her are numerous in both the Eastern and Western churches. She had a special popularity in the Germanic countries.

The chapel of the Santa Bárbara Presidio had a statue of her and requested a painting. The mission received a large painting in 1787 and it may be the one by José de Alcíbar, dated 1785, which now hangs in the Presidio Chapel after it had been found in the basement of the rectory of Our Lady of Sorrows. It appears to have moved back and forth from the mission to the presidio. The statue on the altar in the mission came in 1791; its silver monstrance was sent after 1834. A stone statue modeled on this was carved by an Indian for placement in a niche in the gable of the church facade where it was installed in 1820. A small painting of the saint was on a side altar at Mission San Antonio while a large painting had been sent to San Gabriel mission in 1805. It may be the painting of Saint Ursula by Juan Correa sent as a substitute because it has a tower in the background. Perhaps it was assumed that no one would know the difference!

SAINT BARBARA by José de Alcíbar, 1785, sent to Mission Santa Bárbara in 1787 from Mexico; SB Royal Presidio Chapel

# Santa Inés, Virgen y Mártir

Santa Inés, Virgen y Mártir, Saint Agnes, Virgin and Martyr, was chosen as the patron of the nineteenth California mission, founded on September 17, 1804, by the Father Presidente Fray Esteban Tapis.

Agnes was a Roman maiden who was martyred at the age of twelve or thirteen either around 304 during the persecutions of the Emperor Diocletian or, perhaps, half a century earlier. The oldest versions of her Life are contradictory, but all speak of her resolve to maintain her virginity as a spouse of Christ. According to one version she was taken to a brothel, but a miraculous growth of hair covered her nakedness. Then after her refusal to offer incense to the pagan idols she was put into a fire but remained untouched by the flames. She then was beheaded. Her body was placed in a grave in a catacomb on the Via Nomentana outside of Rome. In the time of Constantine, the first Christian emperor, a basilica was built above her tomb. This was replaced in the seventh century by the structure now standing. At her feast on the 21st of January two lambs are blessed, and their wool is used to make the palliums of the new archbishops of the year.

Her cult enjoyed wide popularity from soon after her death, and she was venerated for her purity. The earliest representation of her, shown as a girl with her hands outstretched in prayer, is on a marble slab from her basilica. The seventh-century mosaic in the apse of the church shows her dressed as a Byzantine princess with flames at her feet. In the church of Sant' Apollinare Nuovo in Ravenna, built by Justinian in the sixth century, Agnes appears in the great mosaic frieze among the virgin martyrs with a lamb at her feet. The lamb, *agnus* in Latin, in fact, became her symbol, and she usually is shown carrying a lamb and sometimes either a palm or a sword, referring to the method of her martyrdom. Jusepe Ribera, in a famous painting in Dresden, shows her with her miraculous growth of hair while in the brothel. A baroque statue of her amidst the flames is on an altar in the church of Sant'Agnese on Piazza Navona above the supposed site of her martyrdom.

A large painting at Mission Santa Inés of the saint carrying the lamb and both a palm and a lily is signed Andrés López, 1803; it may be the painting requested in 1804 and sent in 1805. However, nothing is known of the provenance of the painting of her martyrdom now at the mission. It appears to be a seventeenth-century piece, perhaps after a work by a follower of Pietro da Cortona. Also there is no documentation for the statue in the niche above the altar in the church. It is a typical work of the late eighteenth century in Mexico and had been modified some time during the last century with parts being cut away. It was restored in 1953.

STA YNES VN MR

SAINT AGNES
by Andrés López,
1803, sent to
Mission Santa
Ines in 1805;
Santa Inés
Mission Museum

# La Purísima Concepción de María Santísima

The Virgin Mary, under the appellation of La Purísima Concepción de María Santísima, the Most Pure (or Immaculate) Conception of Mary Most Holy was chosen as the patron of the eleventh of the California missions. It was founded on her feast day, December 8th, 1787, and was thus the second of the three missions which were founded on the feast day of their patron. It was also the first of the two missions dedicated to Mary, the Mother of Jesus.

The Immaculate Conception signifies that Mary was conceived without the blemish of original sin since she was destined to give earthly birth to the second person of the Trinity in the form of Jesus. There is no reference to hers being a virgin birth, and she was physically conceived and born in the same fashion as all mortals. A pious legend in the Middle Ages held that she had been conceived when Joachim met his wife Anna at the Golden Gate in Jerusalem and planted a kiss on her cheek, but this was never an official position of the Church. The exact nature of the Immaculate Conception was disputed, often bitterly, for many centuries and support was especially strong among the Franciscans and in Spain. The Franciscans chose her as special patron and she held that position in the California missions as well. The dogma was finally proclaimed by Pope Pius IX in 1854.

The typical representation of the Immaculate Conception does not seem to have been established until well into the sixteenth century. Before then the embrace of Joachim and Anna at the Golden Gate stood as a symbol for it. The iconography of the type had its fullest development in Spain; Juan de Juanes's paintings of about 1578 in the Jesuit church in Valencia established the type. Her pose, standing with her hands in prayer, derives from the traditional painting of the Assumption of Mary but adds the crescent moon below, and the figure is accompanied by similes from the Litany of Loreto, mostly taken from the Song of Solomon. She is usually dressed in white with a blue cloak. The iconographical type also refers to the beginning of the twelfth chapter of the Book of Revelations: "And there appeared a great wonder in heaven, a woman clothed in the sun, and the moon under her feet, and upon her head a crown of twelve stars." Practically all of the artists in Spain produced versions, though those of Murillo were the most famous. The representation of Our Lady of Guadalupe is an aspect of the Immaculate Conception and is one of the earliest examples of the type.

Because of her special position as patroness of California the Immaculate Conception, whether statue, painting, or print, would have been found in all of the missions. A large number of statues still survive, often on the main altar, and one can cite those now at San Luis Rey (perhaps from the San Diego Presidio), San Juan Capistrano, San Gabriel, San Buenaventura, Santa Bárbara, San Luis Obispo, San Antonio, San Carlos Borromeo, and San Francisco. However, perhaps none of the paintings of the subject now in the missions were there in mission days with the exception of paintings of Our Lady of Guadalupe such as those at San Buenaventura and San Carlos.

THE IMMACULATE CONCEPTION,
18th century Mexican, once in San
Diego, now at Mission San Luis Rey.

# San Luis Obispo de Tolosa

San Luis Obispo de Tolosa, Saint Louis Bishop of Toulouse, was chosen as patron of the fifth mission which was founded on September 1st, 1772.

Louis was born in 1274 at Brignoles in Provence in southern France, the second son of Charles II of Anjou, King of Naples, and Mary the daughter of King Stephen V of Hungary. His uncle was Saint Louis IX King of France and his mother's great-aunt was Saint Elizabeth of Hungary. He was also related to Saint Ferdinand King of Spain. He and his two younger brothers were sent as hostages to Barcelona in exchange for his father who had been defeated and captured in a naval battle. During the seven years of captivity the young princes were instructed by Franciscan friars. Louis absorbed his training well and resolved to join the order. After his release he renounced his claim to succession in favor of his brother Robert and took the habit in Rome in 1296; at the end of the year he was consecrated Bishop of Toulouse. He was much revered for his holiness, but he died of a fever within a few months at the age of twenty-three. He was canonized in 1317. He was buried first in Marseilles, but subsequently his remains were moved to Valencia and now rest in the cathedral there.

The first representation of him, by Simone Martini, was done for his canonization and shows him seated with a magnificent cope over his humble Franciscan habit. He wears a bishop's mitre and holds the crozier while he offers a crown to his kneeling brother Robert of Anjou. A number of paintings of him attest to his popularity for a century or so. A superb gilded statue was made by Donatello in Florence a little over a century later. After the fifteenth century he is rarely represented.

His cult remained largely a purely Franciscan one, and few images of him are found outside of their churches. In California the only surviving ones from the Spanish and Mexican eras are a painting and a statue at his mission. Through a bit of confusion Father Serra had ordered one for the mission, but when he brought it to the Fathers there in 1774 he found that they already had one and were not interested in another one. It ended up in the church at San Carlos and it was still there at the time of the inventory taken in 1834. The painting at San Luis Obispo is possibly by the hand of José de Páez who furnished a number of paintings to the California missions in this period, but it is unsigned. The statue of the saint now on the altarpiece is the one which came in 1791; its bracket presumably came with it, though the canvas altarpiece that came the same year disappeared long ago.

S.<sup>N</sup> LUIS OBISPO.

SAINT LOUIS BISHOP OF TOULOUSE attr. José de Páez, sent to Mission San Luis Obispo before 1774, now in Mission church there

# San Miguel Arcángel

San Miguel Arcángel, Saint Michael the Archangel, was chosen by the Viceroy, the Marquis de Branciforte, to be the patron of the sixteenth mission. It was founded on July 25, 1797, by the Father Presidente, Fray Fermín Francisco de Lasuén. Cabrillo had given the name San Miguel to the Bay of San Diego, but the name was changed by Vizcaíno. San Miguel is the name of one of the Channel Islands and was the patron of a chapel of the Indians at Mission San Buenaventura.

Michael is one of the three archangels mentioned in the scriptures, twice in the Old Testament and twice in the New. He is the protector of the Chosen Peoples, both Christian and Jew, leader of the Heavenly Host against Satan, and protector of Christians at the hour of death. His cult began in the East but spread to the West, especially after he appeared at Monte Gargano in southern Italy in the fifth century.

He is usually shown as a winged warrior subduing the devil. He often has his sword raised and his shield may have the inscription QUIS UT DEUS (who like God). He sometimes carries a set of scales for the weighing of the Soul at death. He appears as a beardless youth of great beauty.

Over the centuries numerous paintings and statues of the archangel have been created. Among the most famous are works by Raphael and Guido Reni which had wide influence. Representations of him are especially common in Mexico and he was a favorite patron for churches. He was featured in theatrical productions from the years following the Conquest and in California he had a leading part in the Pastorela at Christmas time. In 1779 he was chosen as the patron of the California missions.

At least half of the missions in California had painted or carved images of him and some had both. Statues still survive at Carmel, San Antonio, Dolores, Santa Bárbara (two of them), Santa Cruz, and San Miguel. One at Santa Clara was lost in the 1926 fire. A figure now at San Luis Rey comes from San Diego, though there is no documentation to show whether it came from the mission or the presidio. A figure requested by the Fathers at San Buenaventura in 1807 was for the Indians' chapel of San Miguel. Its first site was on the slope of the hill behind the mission buildings named after Monte Gargano in southern Italy. A fine painting from San Antonio now at San Miguel is one of a group of three paintings of archangels while the same three appear in one long canvas in the church at Santa Bárbara. In Mexico and in Peru one often finds sets or groups of seven archangels, but Michael remains the chief among them.

THE ARCHANGEL MICHAEL, 18th century Mexican painting, formerly at Mission San Antonio, now at Mission San Miguel.

# San Antonio de Padua

San Antonio de Padua, Saint Anthony of Padua (Padova in northern Italy), was chosen patron of the third mission which Fray Junípero Serra founded on July 14, 1771 in the Valley of the Oaks. San Antonio was the patron of the Asistencia of San Antonio de Pala as well, established by Fray Antonio Peyri of Mission San Luis Rey. San Antonio was also the patron of one of the first supply ships at the beginning of the colonization of California.

Anthony was born in Lisbon, Portugal, in 1195. Son of a knight of the court of King Alfonso II, he was baptized Ferdinand. He felt his vocation at an early age and first joined the Augustinian order. Subsequently he transferred to the Franciscans in 1221 and then assumed the name Anthony. After an unsuccessful trip to Morocco he landed in Italy and took part in a general chapter of the order in Assisi the same year. Soon he demonstrated a remarkable ability as a preacher and his fame for this and for good works quickly spread. Numerous miracles attributed to him in his lifetime led to his being called "Wonderworker." He died in 1231 and was canonized the following year, one of the most rapid canonizations in the history of the Church. He is a particular patron of the poor and is invoked for the return of lost articles. The basilica built over his remains in Padua is one of the most popular sanctuaries in Italy.

In painting and sculpture he is most frequently shown with a book and a lily and he either holds the Christ Child or it appears to him. Traditionally the Christ Child is said to have appeared to him bodily. However, this and other popular legends are lacking in the first *Life* of him written soon after his death. In fact, the Christ Child is not shown with him until the sixteenth century after which time it becomes standard. The representations of the saint are innumerable; painters as distinguished as Titian and sculptors as notable as Donatello executed cycles representing his miracles. The tradition in Italy was transferred to Spain and thence to the New World unchanged.

Practically every mission in California possessed one or more images of Saint Anthony in canvas or in the round and often both and in all sizes. In perhaps a half of the missions he had a place on the main altar, while in others he had a place above a side altar. After Christ and the Virgin Mary his was the most popular devotion in Hispanic California, and his popularity remains as strong today. A surprisingly large number of both paintings and sculptures have survived. The finest of the paintings is that by José de Páez which now hangs in the church at San Miguel but was sent to Mission San Antonio in 1774.

SAINT ANTHONY OF PADUA, 18th century Mexican statue on the main altar of Mission San Miguel

# Nuestra Señora Dolorosísima de la Soledad

Nuestra Señora Dolorosísima de la Soledad, Our Most Sorrowful Lady of Solitude was chosen as the patron of the thirteenth mission. It was founded October 9, 1791, in the valley of the same name discovered by Portolá's expedition in 1769. It was the second of the two California missions dedicated to the Virgin Mary.

This is Mary the Mother of Jesus after His painful death by Crucifixion. She now feels the sorrow and loneliness after the loss and prayerfully meditates on the events which had just taken place. The Virgin of Solitude is a Spanish variation, along with Nuestra Señora de las Angustias, Our Lady of Anguish, of the Virgin of Sorrows, Nuestra Señora de los Dolores or la Madre Dolorosa. Its origin goes back to Queen Juana who lamented the death of her husband, Philip I, King of Spain, in 1506. It refers more specifically to Mary's solitude on Holy Saturday. For all of these Mary is shown wearing black or dark blue and may have her chest pierced by one or seven swords representing her sorrows.

The Sorrowing Virgin as an independent devotional figure does not appear commonly in Spain before the seventeenth century. At first it is more frequent in sculpture than in painting. There are especially powerful works of striking realism, most notably in Andalusia. The devotion is perhaps strongest on an individual level, and it appealed especially to those who could identify with her sorrows through personal experience. Not surprisingly it found ready acceptance in Mexico. However, the feast only became universal by a papal decree in 1727.

In California representations of the Virgin of Solitude are not very common while practically every mission had one or more of the Virgin of Sorrows, whether in sculpture or in painting, and some had multiple images. At San Antonio there was a Virgen de las Angustias. The representations of all of these differ so little that unless there is a title attached to the image one cannot be sure. The dressed figure of the Virgin once at Mission Soledad and now in the Presidio Chapel in Monterey is called both Virgin of Solitude and Virgin of Sorrows in different documents. Fine statues are at San Luis Rey (from San Diego), Santa Bárbara, Santa Inés, and Santa Cruz. Paintings of Our Lady of Sorrows are most commonly half-length. The most historically important one of these figured in the first conversions at Mission San Gabriel; unfortunately it was stolen some years ago and has not been retrieved.

OUR LADY OF SOLITUDE, 18th century Mexican statue, dressed, originally at Mission La Soledad, now in the Presidio Chapel, Monterey.

# San Carlos Borromeo

San Carlos Borromeo, Saint Charles Borromeo, was chosen patron of the second mission which was founded June 3, 1771, most probably as a gesture to honor Carlos III, King of Spain. The presidio of Monterey was also under the protection of the same saint.

Charles was born of noble parents in the town of Arona in Lombardy in northern Italy in 1583. His mother was Margherita de' Medici, sister to the future Pius IV. As a boy Charles showed an inclination to the religious life, and when his uncle became pope in 1559 the twenty-one-year-old youth was summoned to Rome and was given the cardinal's hat as a layman since he was not ordained and became Papal Secretary of State. This was a perfect example of nepotism which had characterized the days leading up to the Protestant Reformation. However, he proved worthy of the appointment as he was a brilliant administrator and lived a humble and austere life. He was very active in putting into action the reforms of the Council of Trent which was reconvened in 1562. Two years before he had been nominated archbishop of Milan, but he was not consecrated bishop until he had renounced his right to the family title and had been ordained a priest in 1563. He effectively reformed the administration of the archdiocese and cleansed the various religious orders of notable abuses, even at some danger to his life. He showed a great concern for the poor and the sick and mobilized forces to contain the terrible plague of 1576 and visited the sick himself. Although a secular priest he was a member of the Third Order of Saint Francis. He died in 1584 after a life of exemplary piety and humility. He was canonized in 1610; his feast day is November 4th.

He inspired numerous works of painting and sculpture by artists of note, especially in Italy, in the decades following his death. Most striking is a colossal bronze statue of him at Arona overlooking Lago Maggiore. He is usually shown dressed as an archbishop or cardinal with mitre or cardinal's hat and crozier or staff. He is very rare in Spanish and Spanish Colonial art.

In California his images were limited to Monterey and Carmel. In the Presidio Chapel at Monterey there appears once to have been a statue in a niche, while at Carmel there had been two paintings, now gone, and a statue which was sent in 1791; it now crowns the main altar reredos in the church.

SAINT CHARLES BORROMEO, Mexican statue on high altar sent in 1791 to Mission San Carlos Borromeo.

# Santa Cruz

Santa Cruz, the Holy Cross, was the name given to the twelfth mission founded August 28th, 1791, on a site so named by the Portolá expedition in 1769.

The Cross on which Jesus Christ died is the most holy and enduring of all Christian symbols. It did not come into common use, however, until the time of the Roman Emperor Constantine who proclaimed Christianity as the official religion of the Empire in the Edict of Milan in 315. According to tradition the True Cross was found by Constantine's mother, Helena, during a visit to Jerusalem in 326. A portion of the Cross was kept intact and placed in a jeweled silver reliquary. This was stolen by the Persian king Chosroes but was recovered by the Emperor Heraclius II in 628. The Cross was eventually cut into tiny pieces, and these along with other objects of the Crucifixion, the nails, the Crown of Thorns, and the like, became the most precious relics of Christendom. The True Cross seems to have been of the Latin form, and although numerous variations of the Cross are known this is the type which one finds in California, almost without exception.

Throughout the centuries the Christian Cross has been executed in a great variety of materials, and in California it appeared in many sizes and functions. Large wooden crosses were set up at the time of founding of all the missions, and a large cross usually was placed in the cemeteries to serve for all those buried there since no individual markers were placed there. The founding cross often remained opposite the mission church, and that of Santa Clara still survives encased in concrete.

Crosses of wood or wrought iron were placed on the summit of church facades, towers, or domes, and there are crosses carved in relief above doorways at Santa Bárbara and Santa Inés; there was a stucco relief of a cross between flags in one of the bell-towers at Santa Bárbara. Within the church little wooden crosses surmounted the Stations of the Cross and often were placed on the main altar in lieu of a crucifix, especially in the early years of the missions. Some of the latter were of silver while Mission Dolores had a painted and gilded one from Manila and San Diego had one of tortoise shell. The silver one at Carmel had a sliver of wood of the True Cross. We find mention of Jerusalem Crosses which are of the usual form but veneered with engraved mother-of-pearl. One of these was attached to the top of the tabernacle at Mission Santa Bárbara. Wooden crosses were ordered in quantity to be distributed to the neophytes, either to wear or to hang in their dwellings.

There were painted crosses over doorways in the Fathers' dwelling at San Juan Bautista and in the chapel at Pala, over Holy Water fonts at San Luis Rey and Pala, in altarpieces painted on the walls at Pala and Dolores, and along the dado in the chapel at Pala where there were once more than a hundred crosses. An elaborate painted cross over a window in an undated adobe house on Santa Cruz Island may have been painted by a mission-trained artist.

THE HOLY CROSS: Christ under the Cross, painted early 19th century by Indian neophytes at Mission San Fernando, now at Mission San Gabriel

# San Juan Bautista

San Juan Bautista, Saint John the Baptist, was chosen by the Viceroy, the Marquis de Branciforte, as the patron of the fifteenth mission. It was founded by the Father Presidente Fray Fermín Francisco de Lasuén on June 24, 1797, the feast day of the saint.

John, called the Baptist, was the son of Zacharias, a priest in the Temple of Jerusalem, and Elizabeth, a kinswomen of Mary. As a youth he went into the desert to live as a hermit till the age of thirty and then began to preach on the banks of the Jordan against the evils of the time. He urged penance and baptism and soon attracted large crowds. He baptised Christ whom he recognized as the Messiah; he spoke of Him as the Lamb of God. He was arrested by Herod Antipas for political motives and was beheaded at the request of Salome, the daughter of Herodias, the wife of Herod.

From earliest times he had held a preeminent position with the church. Scenes of Baptism appear in the Catacombs in Rome, and the iconography is among the earliest of Christian stories to be established; it has varied little since then. John has unruly hair and a beard and usually wears an animal skin. In the Eastern church he also often accompanies Christ and the Virgin in the grouping known as the Deësis, or he may be a single isolated figure as well.

In the West, in statuary or painting, he is usually shown baptising Jesus at the River Jordan. He stands on the bank while Jesus is in the water; a dove representing the Holy Spirit descends from above. As an isolated figure he is often shown preaching and may hold a staff topped with a Cross. He may also carry or be accompanied by a lamb, a reference to Christ as the Lamb of God. Scenes of his beheading are less common, though one can occasionally find sculptures or paintings of his head on a platter.

Most of the missions had paintings of the Baptism of Christ for placement in the baptistry. A number of these paintings survive, including a fine one by José de Páez at San Luis Obispo; it is of the sort that could be rolled up. A single figure of the saint with a lamb is on the main altar at San Juan Bautista. Another one of uncertain provenance, probably Mission San Diego or the presidio of San Diego, is now at San Luis Rey; it has lost its Lamb which would have been carried. A small painting of the saint kneeling with a lamb in front of a Cross at San Juan Bautista may be one sent in 1805. The young John resting in the desert, a subject more common in Italian than Spanish painting, can be seen at Mission Santa Inés.

BAPTISM OF CHRIST BY JOHN THE BAPTIST, 18th cent. Mexican painting sent to Mission San Antonio in 1786; Mission San Miguel

# Santa Clara de Asís

Santa Clara de Asís, Saint Clare of Assisi, had been chosen as the patron of the eighth mission by the Viceroy Bucareli: it was founded on January 12th, 1771. Santa Clara was also chosen as the name for a river in southern California, near present-day Ventura, given by Fr. Crespi in 1769.

Clare was born in Assisi in the Umbrian region of central Italy in 1194 of noble parents. She showed a pious leaning from childhood, refusing to marry at twelve a wealthy suitor chosen by her father. She was so impressed by a Lenten sermon of Saint Francis in 1212 that she left home and took the Franciscan habit from the saint at the Porziuncula. He placed her in a convent of Benedictine nuns, but she eventually founded her own order, the Poor Clares, modeled on that of Saint Francis. She was soon joined by her sister Agnes and in 1215 she moved to San Damiano where she remained as superior of the convent for forty years. Her mother, another sister, and several noble ladies came to the convent as well. Her rule was as austere as that of Saint Francis, if not more so. In particular, she insisted on absolute poverty, and as the order remained cloistered they were dependent on the charity of the mendicant Franciscan friars. The order flourished and other convents were established. Her prayers were credited with saving Assisi from siege by the soldiers of the Emperor Frederick II. On one occasion she caused attacking soldiers to flee by holding up the monstrance with the Blessed Sacrament. She died in 1253 and was canonized in 1255. After her death a church was built for her in Assisi. Her remains were hidden deep beneath the floor and were discovered only in 1850.

She is usually shown with a brown Franciscan habit with a shoulder length black veil. In early representations she carries a sceptre-like cross, a lily, or a book. In later centuries she is usually shown with a monstrance and the staff of an abbess. Her representations tend to be limited to Franciscan churches whether for nuns or friars.

The mission of Santa Clara had a number of representations of the saint, both in painting and in sculpture. There are two statues mentioned in the 1851 inventory when the mission was turned over to the Jesuits for a college. A carved and painted figure in the sacristy apparently soon disappeared, but a dressed figure remained on the main altar until it was lost in the 1926 fire. It apparently had been there since the founding, but a new brown robe for it had come in 1840. A large painting of the saint had arrived by 1782. The saint also was represented in a painting on the facade of the church done in 1835 or 1836, probably by Agustin Dávila. A statue, no longer extant, was on a side altar at Carmel, and there is a figure on the main altar at Dolores. A painting at La Purísima was possibly lost in the 1812 earthquake. At Santa Bárbara there is a fine large painting in the church showing three Franciscan female saints with Saint Clare in the center. It is first identified in the 1834 inventory but could be among several unidentified paintings which had arrived in earlier years.

SAINT CLARE OF ASSISI, detail from an 18th century Mexican painting of three Franciscan female saints in the Church of Mission Santa Bárbara.

# San José

San José, Saint Joseph, was chosen as the patron of the fourteenth mission by the Viceroy, the Marquis de Branciforte. It was founded on June 11, 1797 by the Father Presidente Fray Fermín Francisco de Lasuén.

Joseph, spouse of the Virgin Mary and foster father of Jesus, is mentioned in the first and second books of Matthew and Luke in the New Testament which tell of the infancy and early childhood of Christ. He was said to have been a builder or a carpenter, and he is described as a just man. The time of his death is not recorded, though he was presumably older than the Virgin Mary. According to one tradition he was already an elderly man when they married, but there is no documentary source for this, and in Hispanic countries he usually has dark hair rather than grey as is common elsewhere. He was venerated in the East from early times, but his popularity in the West comes later. His feast was only introduced into the Roman calendar in 1479. His popularity coincides with the discovery and colonization of the New World. The church of San José de los Naturales in Mexico City-Tenochtitlán was among the first churches in the Roman Catholic world to be dedicated to him. He, in fact, became a special patron of the converted Indians. He was declared patron of the Universal Church by Pope Pius IX in 1870. Subsequently he became a protector of workers and patron of social justice.

Until the end of the sixteenth century Saint Joseph is almost always shown as a participant in scenes such as the Nativity, the Flight into Egypt, and other events mentioned in the scriptures rather than as a single figure for devotional purposes. However, even then we begin to find scenes of the Holy Family and the Death of Saint Joseph. As a devotional figure he normally appears with Jesus either as a baby in his arms or as a child holding on to his hand as in certain versions of the Holy Family. He almost never, until very recent times, appears alone as his importance comes from being the foster father of Jesus. He usually holds a staff, either with lilies signifying his chastity or with flowers that blossomed from his rod when he was chosen as the spouse of the Virgin Mary according to a medieval legend.

His image was to be found at every mission whether in sculpture or painting and numerous examples survive. Statues usually were found on the main altar unless there was a special side altar dedicated to him. He is usually shown carrying the baby Jesus; often one or both figures had crowns. At Carmel there was once a small painting of the Death of Saint Joseph but it has not survived. A fine painting of the Patronage of Saint Joseph at Mission Dolores shows Saint Joseph and the Christ Child adored by King Carlos IV and Pope Pius IV. It must be later than 1788, the year of the king's coronation.

SAINT JOSEPH as Patron with Pope Pius IV and King Carlos IV, late 18th century Mexican painting at Mission Dolores

# San Francisco de Asís

San Francisco de Asís, Saint Francis of Assisi, was chosen as the patron of the sixth of the Franciscan missions in California which was founded on June 26, 1776. According to Paloú in his Life of Serra when the padre presidente asked the Inspector General, Jose de Galvez, why there was no mission for Saint Francis among the first three planned he received the reply, "If Saint Francis wants a mission let him cause his port to be discovered, and it will be placed there." Thus he is the patron of the port, the mission, the presidio, and subsequently of the great city which all bear his name.

Francis was born in 1182 at Assisi in the central Italian region of Umbria. The son of a wealthy merchant, he led a carefree and rather frivolous youth and planned on a career as a soldier, but a number of events changed his outlook, and he gave up his inheritance and began to live a life of poverty. His example soon attracted disciples, and in time he founded the order of the Friars Minor who took vows of poverty, obedience, and chastity. Eventually the order won papal approval. An otherwise unsuccessful trip to Egypt and the Holy Land to convert the Mohammedans resulted in the establishment of a Franciscan foothold in Jerusalem as guardians of the holy places. In 1223 he established the custom of the Christmas crib. He was unique in his time for his appreciation of nature and of all of God's creatures. In 1224 he received the Stigmata, the five wounds of Christ, as a special sign of divine favor. He died in 1226 and was canonized two years later. He is buried in the crypt of the basilica dedicated to him in Assisi.

Typically Saint Francis is shown as bearded with his head tonsured, and he wears a brown robe with a rope as a belt. He usually shows the Stigmata, and he often carries a cross or crucifix and a skull as well. The earliest representation of Francis, in the Benedictine monastery of the Sacro Speco in Subiaco, commemorates his visit there in 1223 and may be a contemporary portrait. The number of representations of him since then is beyond counting. The most important of the cycles of his life is that traditionally attributed to Giotto in the Upper Church of Assisi. Representations in Spain follow Italian models and only towards the end of the sixteenth century does one find a specifically Spanish interpretation in the more meditative works of El Greco and Zurbarán. Mexico followed Spanish models and these, in turn, are what one finds in the California missions. The theme is the penitential one and nowhere are there references to his interest in nature.

All of the missions had either paintings or sculptures of the saint and the latter usually were placed on the altarpieces, often paired with Saint Dominic whom he had met on one of his visits to Rome. A number of original statues and paintings still survive, though the rare paintings mentioned in the records which show him receiving the Stigmata have not come down to us.

SAINT FRANCIS OF ASSISI, 18th century Mexican painting in the church of Mission San Fernando.

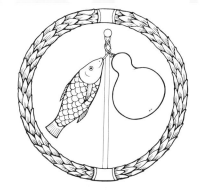

# San Rafael Arcángel

San Rafael Arcángel, Saint Raphael the Archangel, was chosen as the patron of the *asistencia* founded December 14, 1817, across the Golden Gate as a sanitarium for the neophytes of Mission San Francisco. It did not have a resident missionary until 1823 when it was raised to full mission status.

Raphael is one of the three archangels mentioned by name in the scriptures and venerated liturgically. His name means "God heals" so he is an appropriate choice for a place to recover one's health. He appears as one of the protagonists in the Old Testament apocryphal Book of Tobit. A just man, Tobit, who had a son Tobias, had been blinded by the excrement of a sparrow. He decided to send his son to collect a debt at Rages in Media. He was to be accompanied by Raphael, in disguise. When they reached the River Tigris a fish leapt out at Tobias. Tobias caught the fish and Raphael instructed him to cut out the heart, liver, and gall. In time they came to the house of Raguel, the father of Sara whom Tobias was destined to marry. Sara, however, had had seven husbands, all who died before the marriage was consummated because a devil lusted after her. Tobias burned the heart and liver of the fish with ashes of perfume and caused the devil to flee; and this wedding night with Sara ended happily. Afterwards they continued to Media to collect the debt and eventually returned home. There Tobias put the gall on his father's eyes and cured him of blindness. It was after that when Raphael revealed his true identity.

These stories had considerable popularity in art from the fifteenth through the eighteenth centuries, especially those dealing with the catching of the fish and the healing of Tobit's blindness. When represented alone Raphael is dressed as a pilgrim, is winged, and carries a fish and sometimes a traveler's staff with a gourd tied to it.

In the New World paintings and statues of him were frequent, though narrative scenes were quite rare. He was a patron of travelers, a protector against eye trouble as well as other illnesses, and a protector against monsters.

There were several paintings and sculptures of the archangel in the missions, and a number still exist. Quantities of prints and novenas of San Rafael were ordered, but they have not survived. A statue at San Juan Capistrano, sent in 1800, has recently been restored after having been found in fragments in the sacristy of the ruined Old Stone Church. Another, now at San Luis Rey, comes from San Diego, perhaps from the presidio rather than the mission. A large painting of the sort that could be rolled up is now in the replica structure at Mission San Rafael and may be the one mentioned in the annual report of 1818. A fine painting, one of a set of three, now at San Miguel comes from San Antonio. All three archangels appear in one painting in the church at Santa Bárbara. A primitive example at Santa Inés with strongly Indian features is one of the rare neophyte oil paintings on canvas.

THE ARCHANGEL RAPHAEL, 18th century Mexican painting, formerly at Mission San Antonio, now at Mission San Miguel.

# San Francisco Solano

San Francisco Solano, Saint Francis Solanus, was chosen in 1824 as the patron of the mission at the site of Sonoma which had been established on July 4, 1823, as a new site for Mission San Francisco de Asís. The intended move was done without proper authorization and was countermanded with the result that a new mission, the twenty-first, and last, came into being. To emphasize this contemporary records often refer to the mission as San Solano, and sometimes as new San Francisco.

Francis Solanus was born at Montilla, the home of the famous Amontillado sherry, south of Córdova in Spain, in 1549 of noble parents. He joined the Franciscan order in his twentieth year and was ordained a priest seven years later. Subsequently he was sent as master of novices to Arrizafa. He was noted for his preaching but was also an accomplished violinist. In 1598 he went to South America as a missionary and was active in Peru, Tucumán, and Paraguay. He was a remarkable linguist and quickly learned the Indian dialects so that he might preach in them. He eventually returned to Lima where he was superior of the local monastery. He died in 1610. He was beatified in 1675 and canonized in 1726. He is considered to be the Apostle of South America.

He is usually shown in a Franciscan habit, carrying a Cross. Occasionally he carries a violin. He may be shown baptizing as in a relief on the stone reredos from the military chapel of La Castrense of Santa Fe, New Mexico (now in the church of Cristo Rey), or in a painting given to Mission San Fernando in recent years where he is still called "Blessed." It is a rather provincial Spanish work; none of the converts are Indians. Perhaps it comes from a church in the region of his birthplace. A dressed statue of 1743 in the Monastery of San Francisco in Lima stands on a base decorated with scenes of his life and figures of Indians. A large painting of the saint preaching by José de Páez was one of a series of his life done in 1764 for the lower cloister of the College of San Fernando in Mexico City. It would have been familiar to the Franciscans who came to California, especially Fr. Junípero Serra who was in residence at the college just when the paintings were being done. He was, in fact, entering his teens when Saint Francis Solanus was canonized, and he held him in special esteem. From the beginning he had wished that a mission be founded in his name in California.

A few images of him found their way to California. Paintings at San Carlos and San Francisco Solano disappeared long ago. A painting of him with a violin at Santa Bárbara has recently disappeared. A small figure at Santa Clara was sent there in 1805 and survived the fire of 1926; it is in one of the side chapels. A larger statue on a side altar at San Francisco may have come with the reredos which was sent in 1810.

SAINT FRANCIS SOLANO,
early 19th century Mexican
statue on side altar of
Mission Dolores.

# San Pedro y San Pablo

The Apostles Peter and Paul were chosen as joint patrons of the mission pueblo of San Pedro y San Pablo de Bicuñer, the second of those founded in 1780 on the California side of the Colorado River at the request of the Yuman Indians. Had they succeeded these would have been way stations linking the Franciscan Missions of Sonora and those on the Pacific Coast, but the whole enterprise ended in disaster the following year, and the missions were abandoned.

Simon was a Galilean fisherman who after being a disciple of John the Baptist joined the band of disciples of Jesus along with his brother Andrew. He was the first to acknowledge the divinity of Christ, and Jesus said to him, "Thou art Peter, and it is upon this rock that I will build my church." He was present at many of the miracles but denied Him at the time of Christ's condemnation. He was the first to encounter Him after the resurrection. Peter went on to perform many miracles and eventually was martyred in Rome by being crucified upside down during the Neronian pesecution around 64 A.D. He is revered as the first pope and is called the Prince of the Apostles.

Saul of Tarsus was a devout Jew and a Roman citizen; he chose to change his name to the Latin form Paul. At first a persecutor of the Christians, he was dramatically converted to Christianity during a trip to Damascus. He went on to become the great apostle to the gentiles and traveled throughout Asia Minor and Greece and was even said to have reached Spain. He was in Rome on two occasions; during the second he was martyred by being beheaded in 67 A.D. at a spot on the Via Ostiense.

Peter and Paul have a joint feast day on June 29th. They are often represented together in art. The earliest representation is a bronze medallion with their busts dating from the third century. They are among the most commonly represented of the Apostles in art. Peter is usually shown with a book and a pair of keys, the keys to heaven, while Paul also carries a book and a sword, referring to his martyrdom.

The images of Saints Peter and Paul in the mission church on the Colorado would have been destroyed in the massacre, but those saints had images in a number of the coastal missions. In particular they figured in sets of the Apostles, the *Apostolados*. Two sets at San Gabriel and San Juan Bautista are still extant while others hung at San Juan Capistrano and La Purísima and a fifth was painted on the nave walls at Santa Clara. The fathers at San Buenaventura requested a set in sculpture, but it was not sent. Two separate paintings of the two apostles, now in the side chapel, once adorned the main altar reredos of San Carlos mission, while the two were in a single canvas sent to Mission San Francisco in 1788. This mission also had a small figure of Saint Peter which had come in 1790, and San Fernando was billed for a small wax one in 1810. At Mission San José Fr. Marciso Durán requested that a figure of Saint Peter enthroned and dressed as the pope should be placed on the highest level of the reredos that he ordered (but did not receive) in 1825. At San Gabriel five canvases from a dismembered altarpiece show scenes from the life of Saint Peter while a sixth one from the same source has an incident from the life of Saint Paul. One of the paintings is signed by Jerónimo de la Portilla, an artist active in Puebla in the late seventeenth century.